VOLUME 3

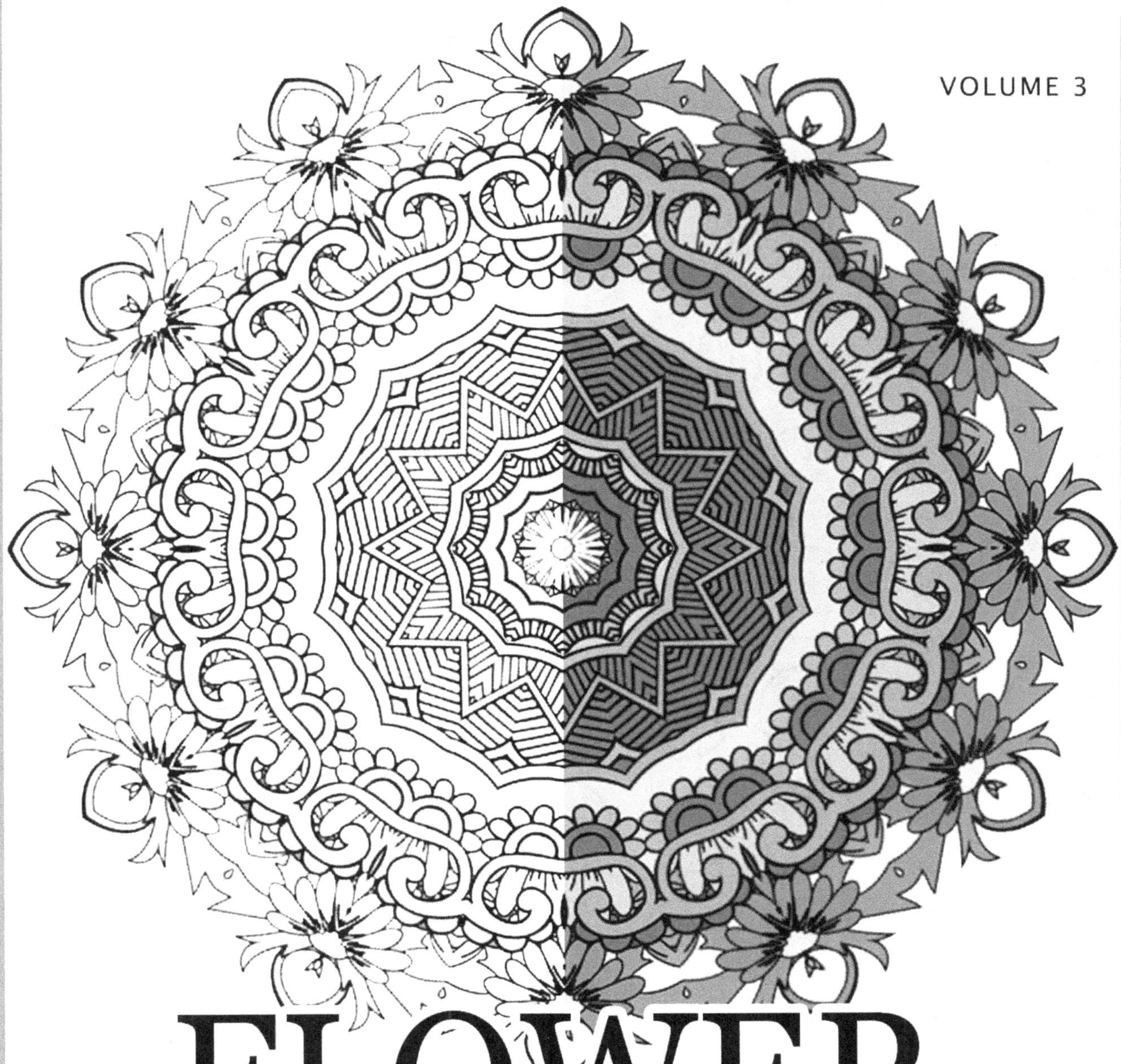

FLOWER
MANDALAS

COLORING BOOK FOR ADULTS

COLOR TEST PAGE

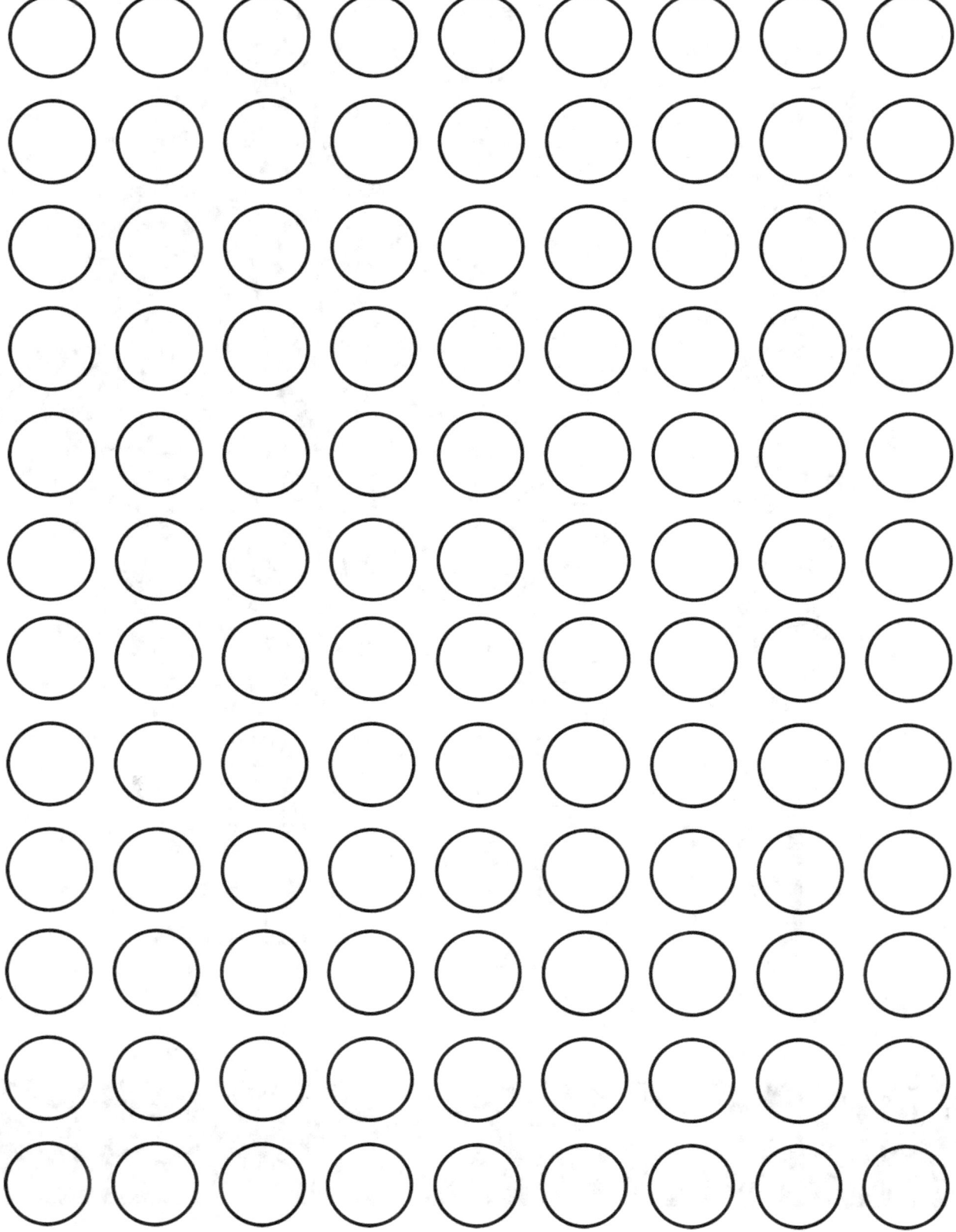

COLOR TEST PAGE

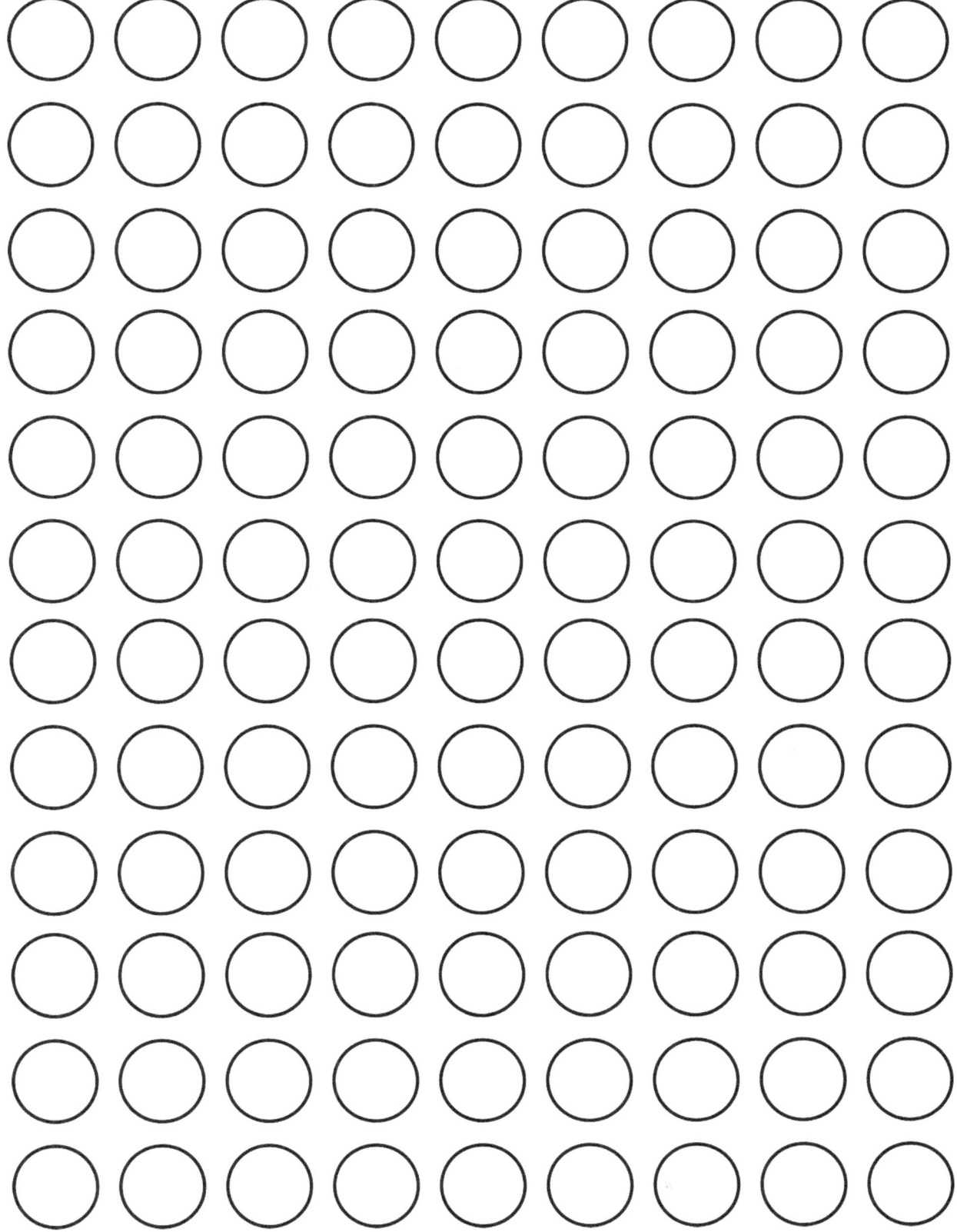

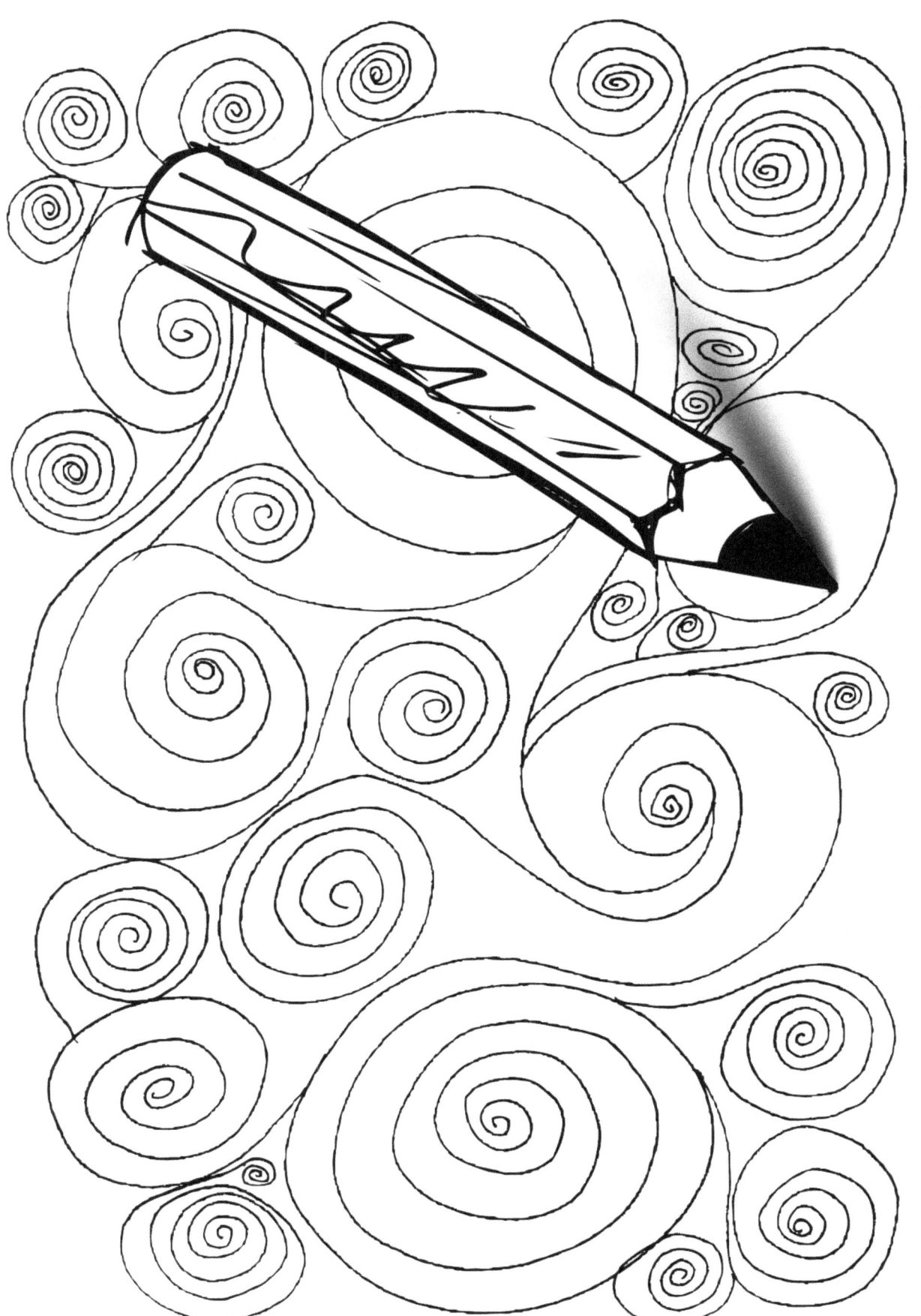

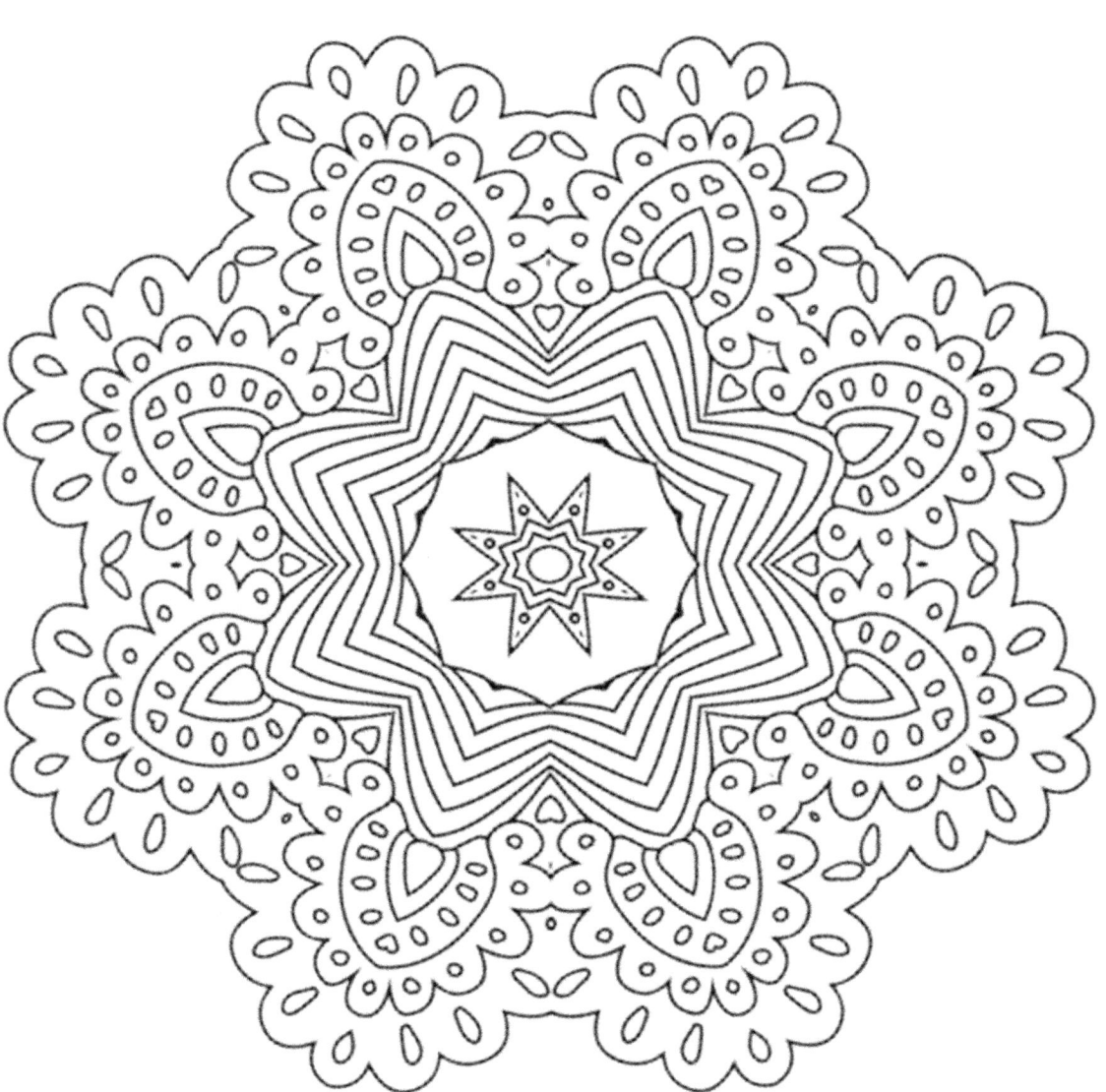

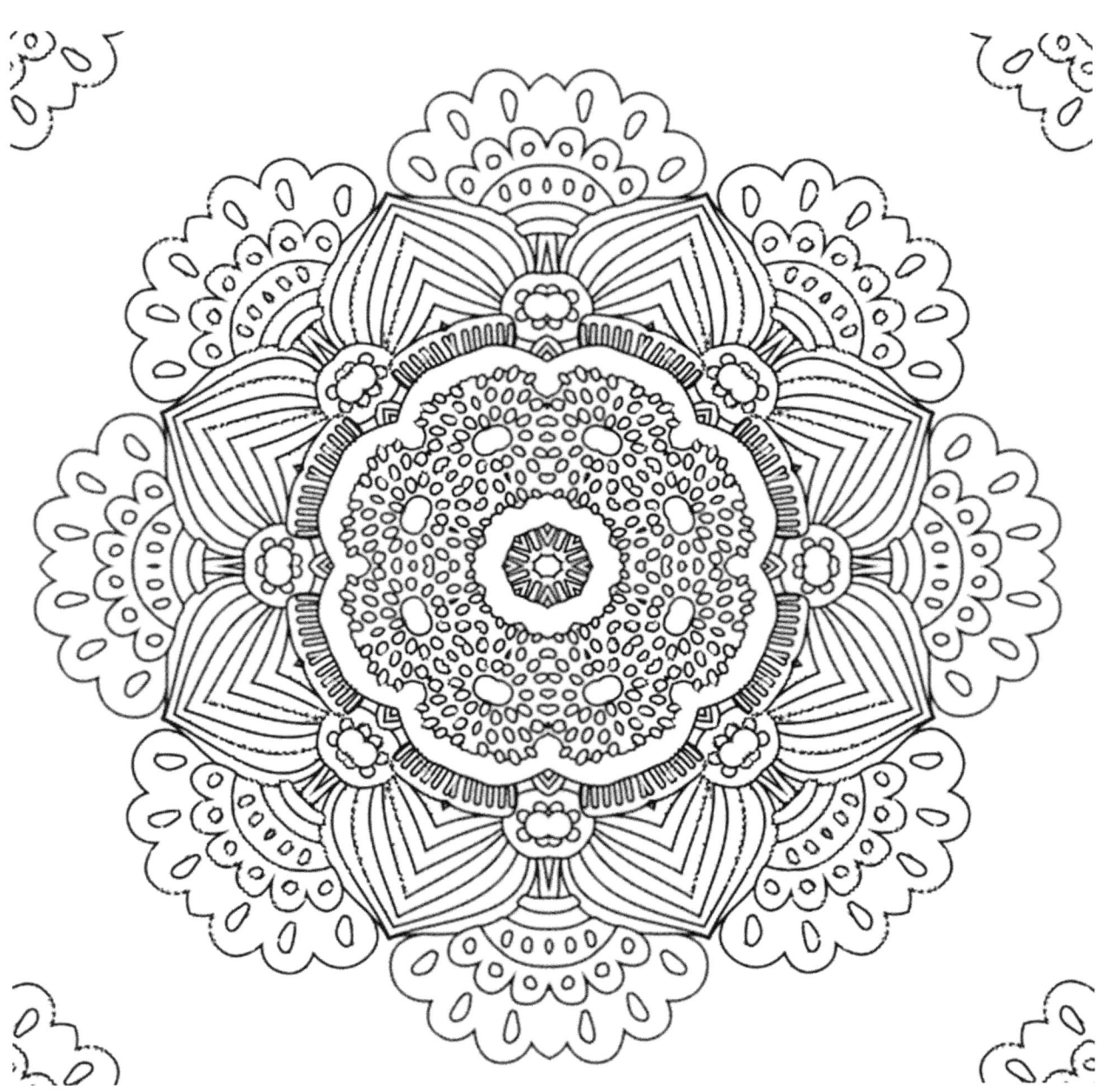

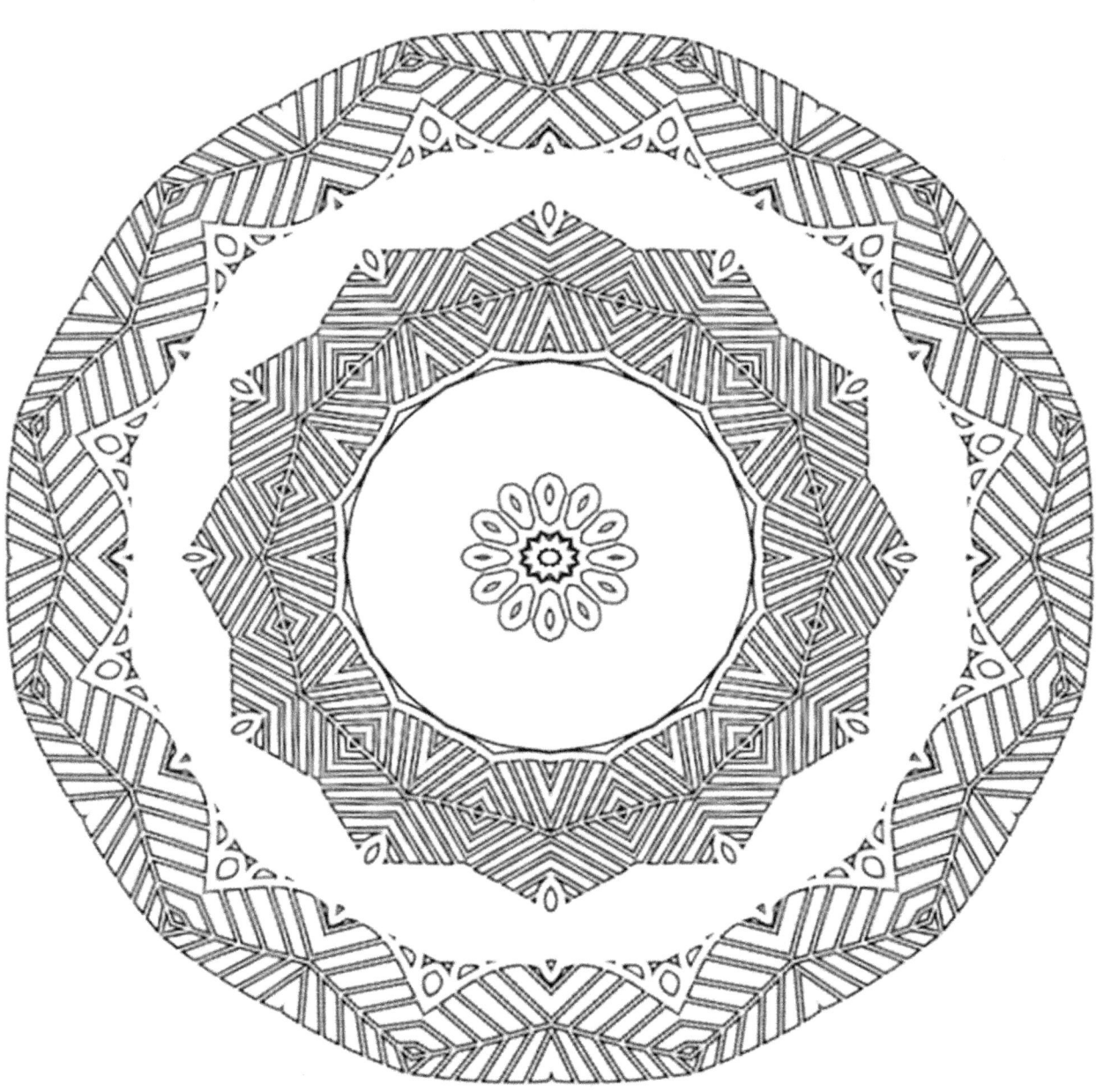

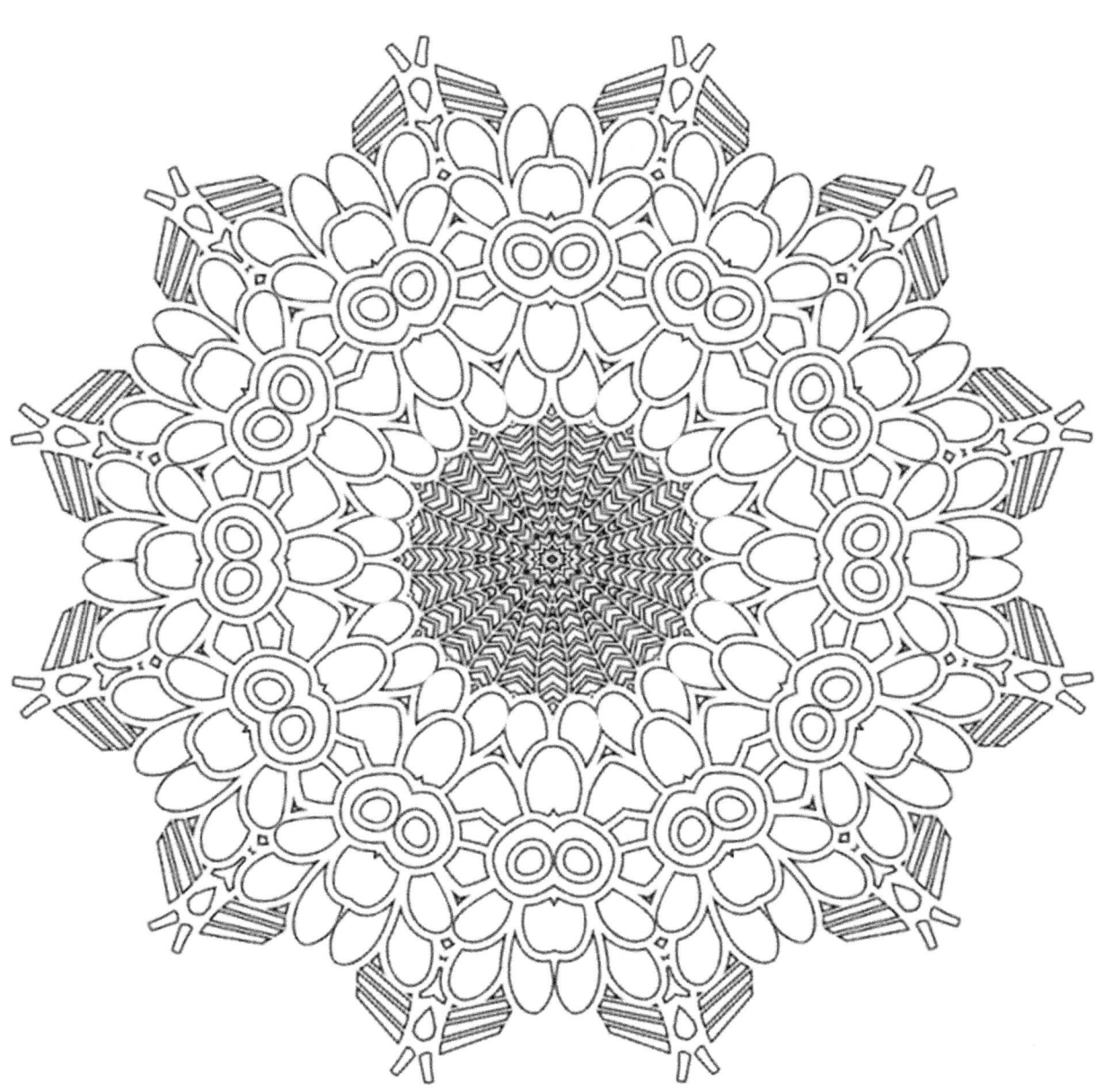

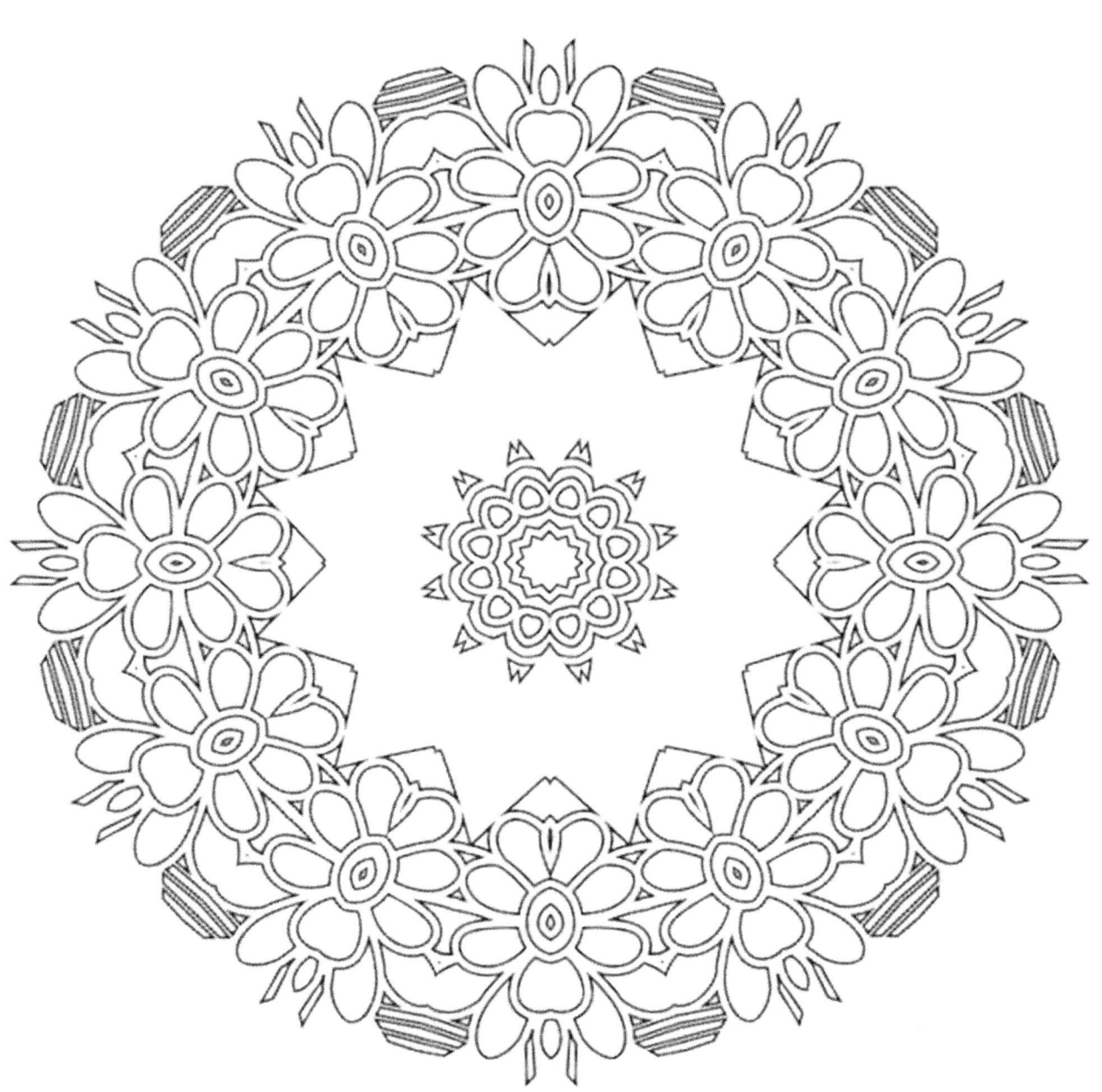

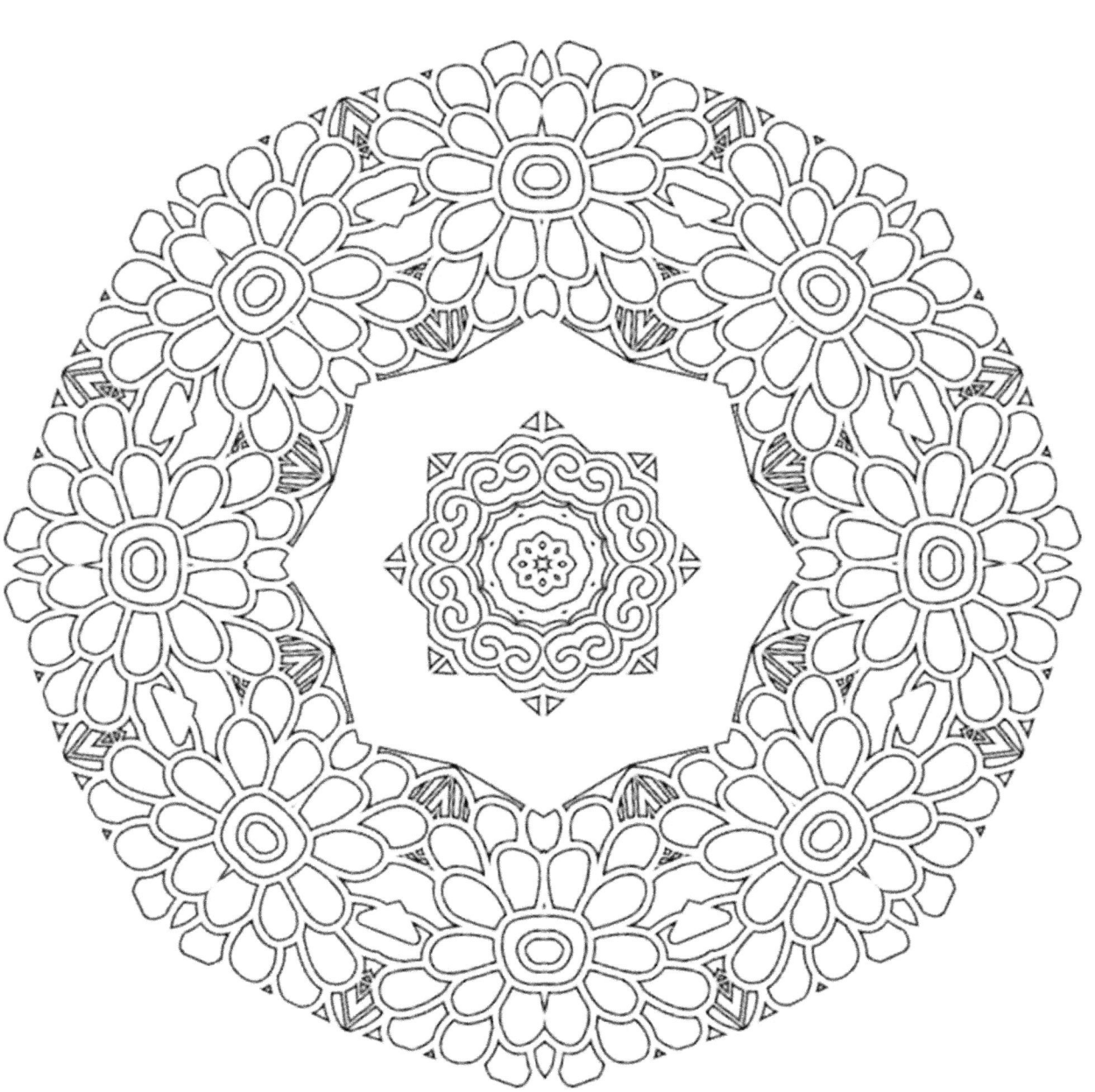

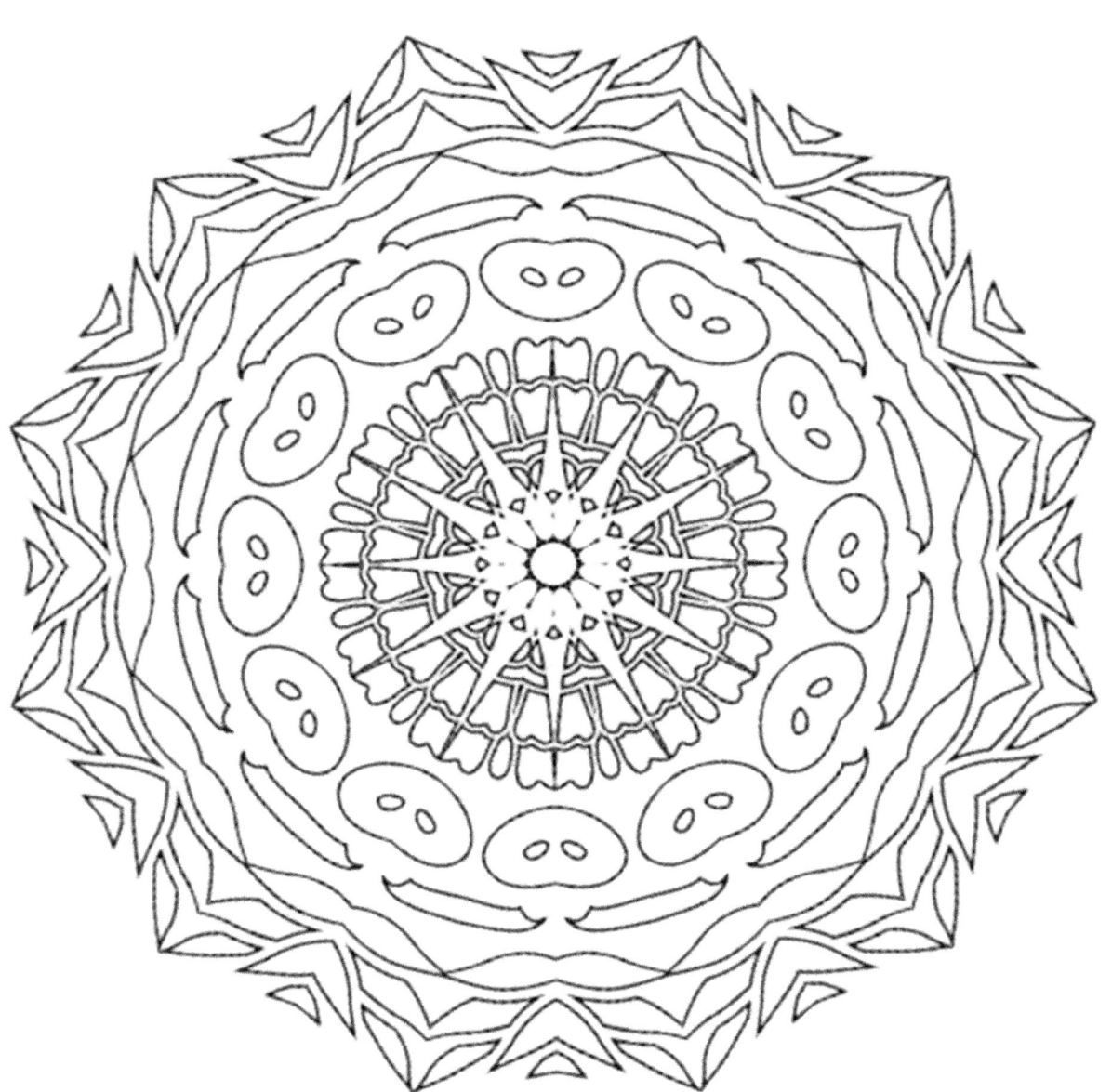

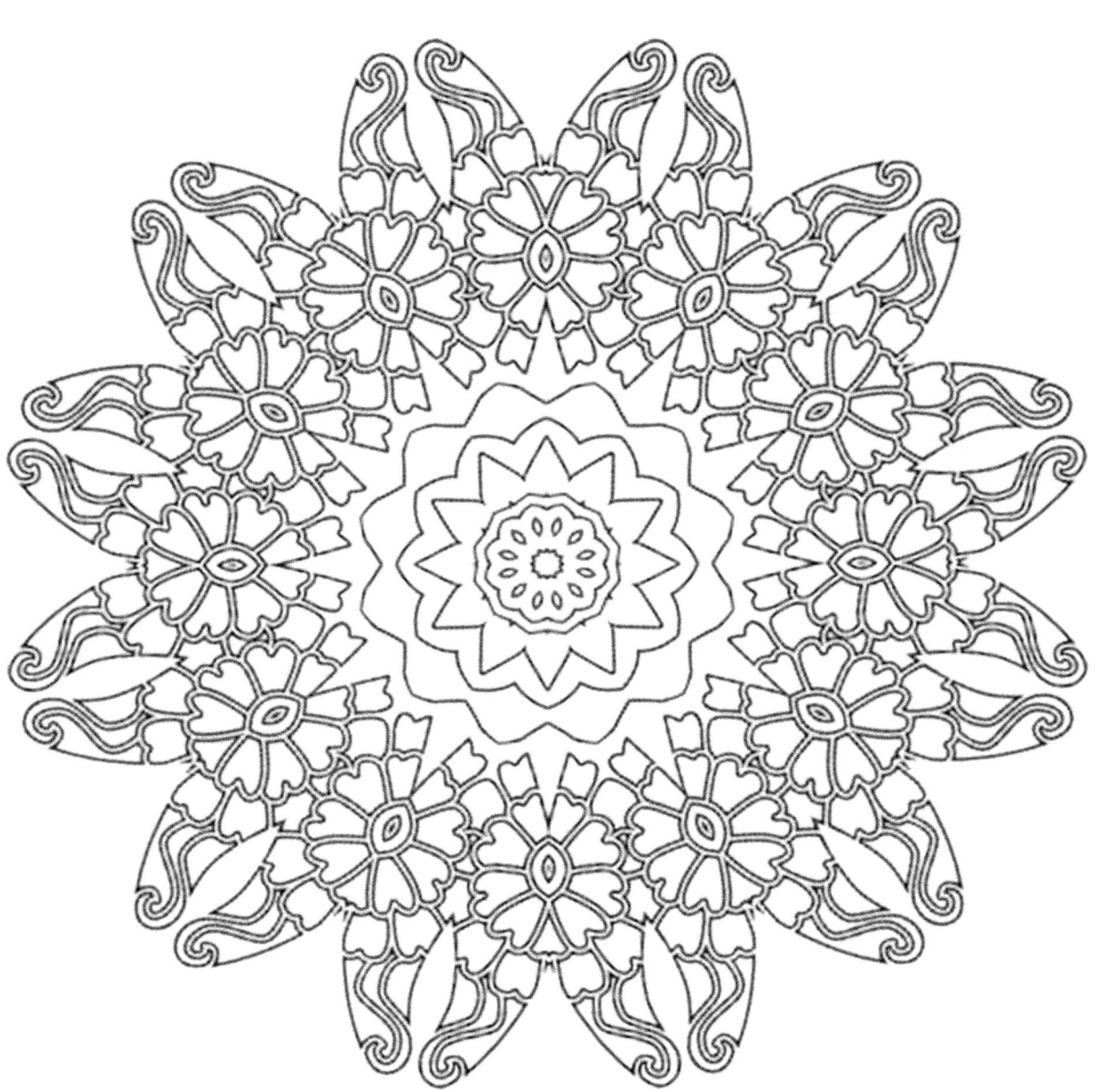

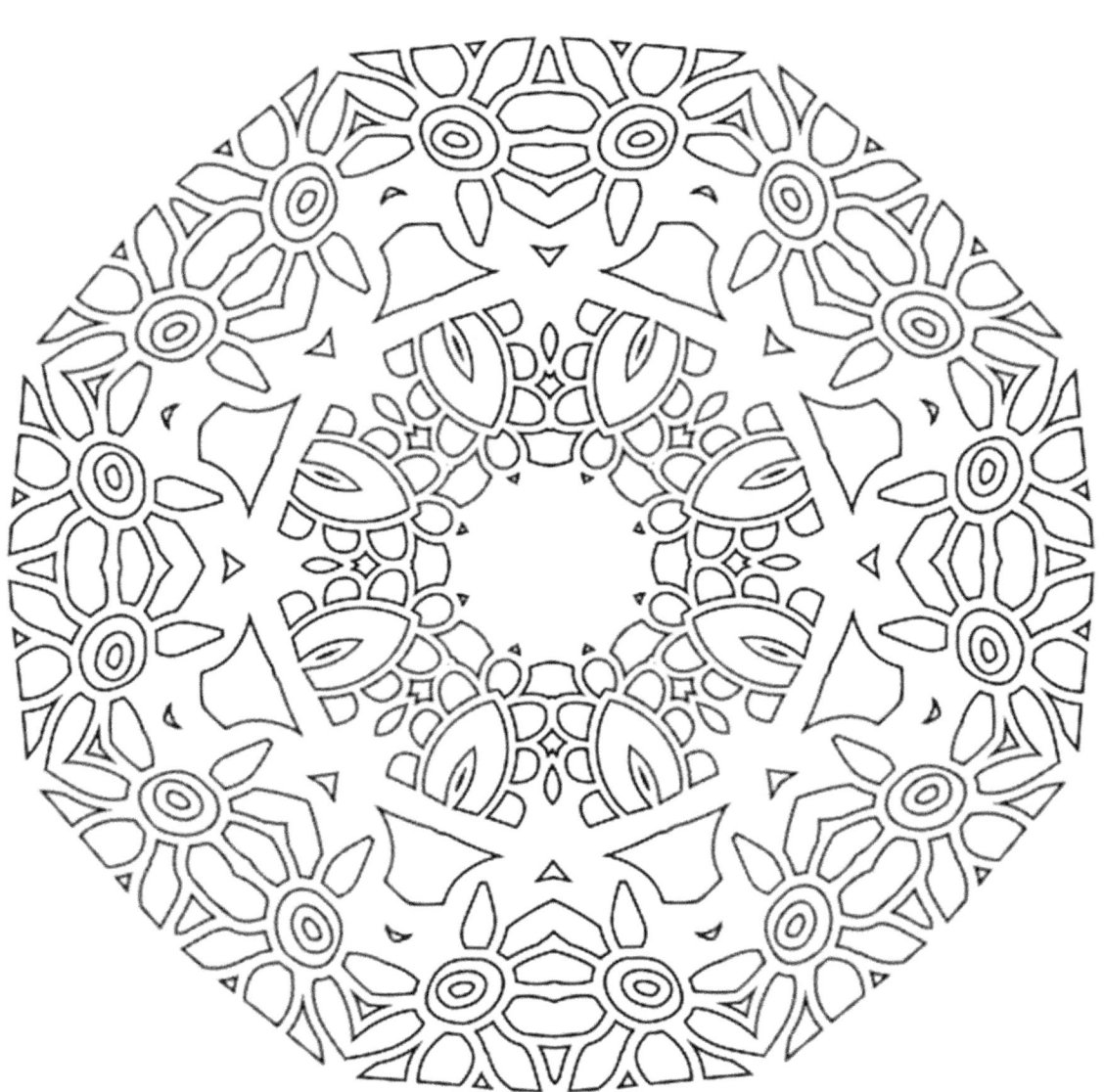

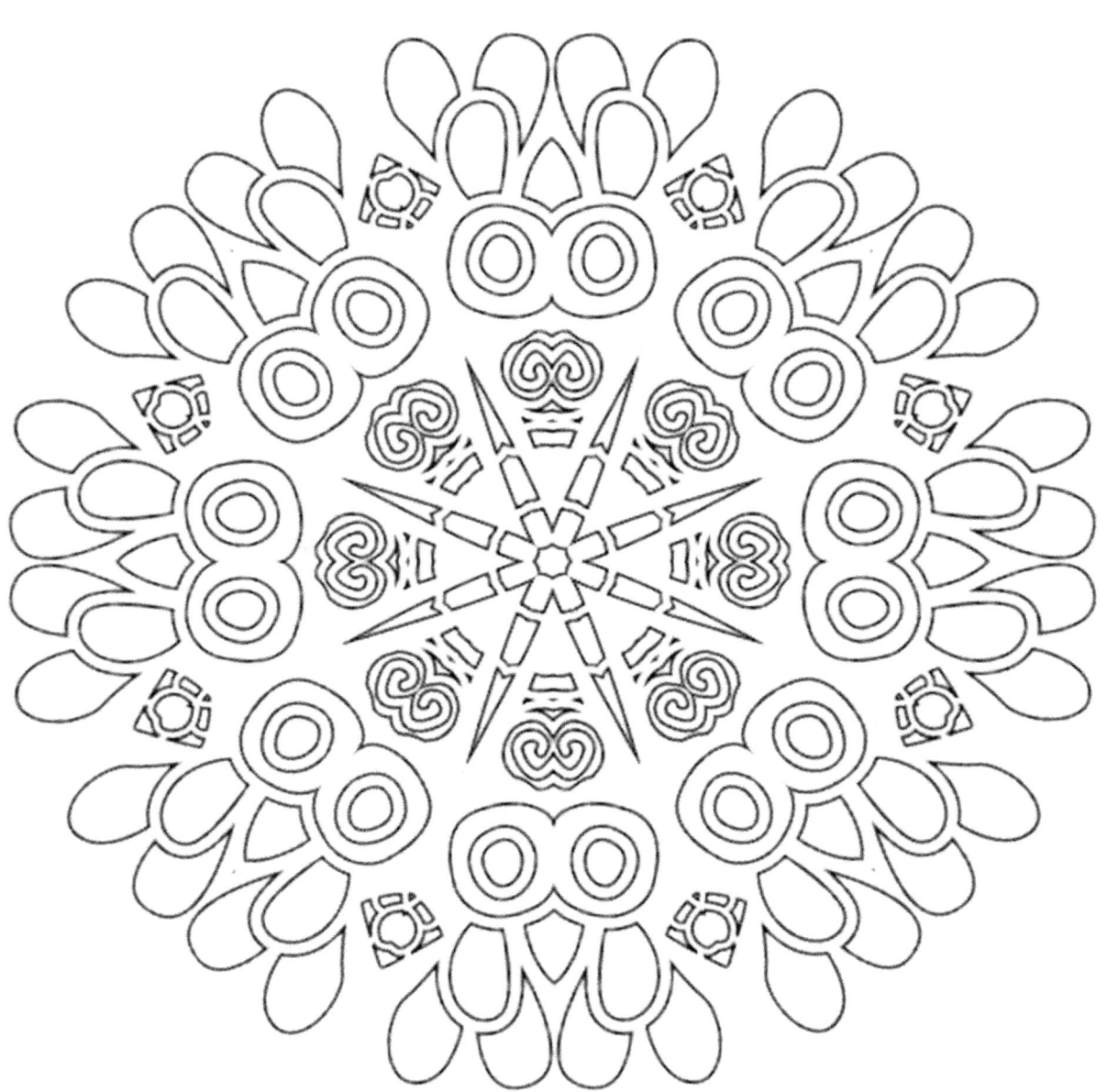

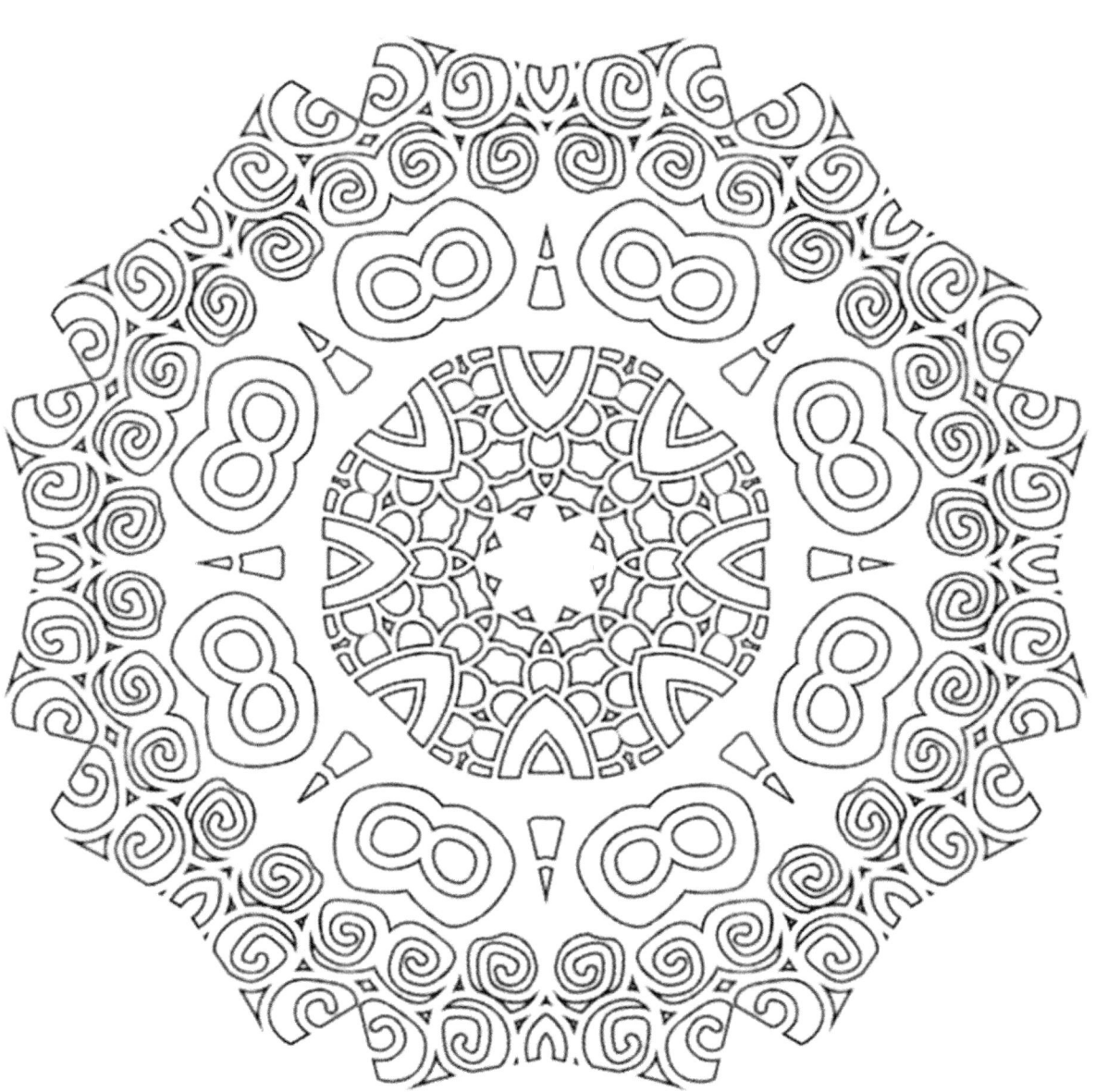

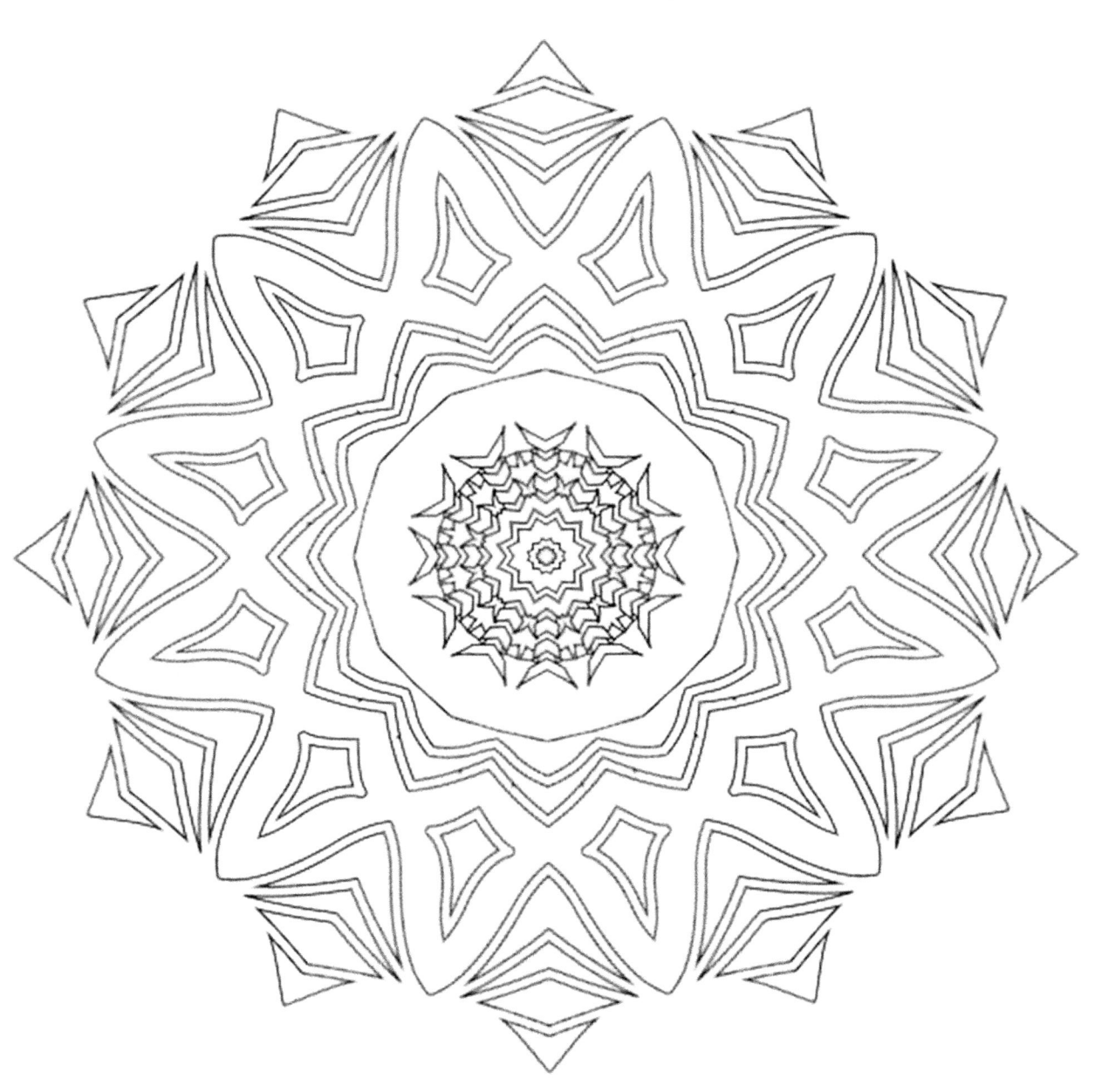

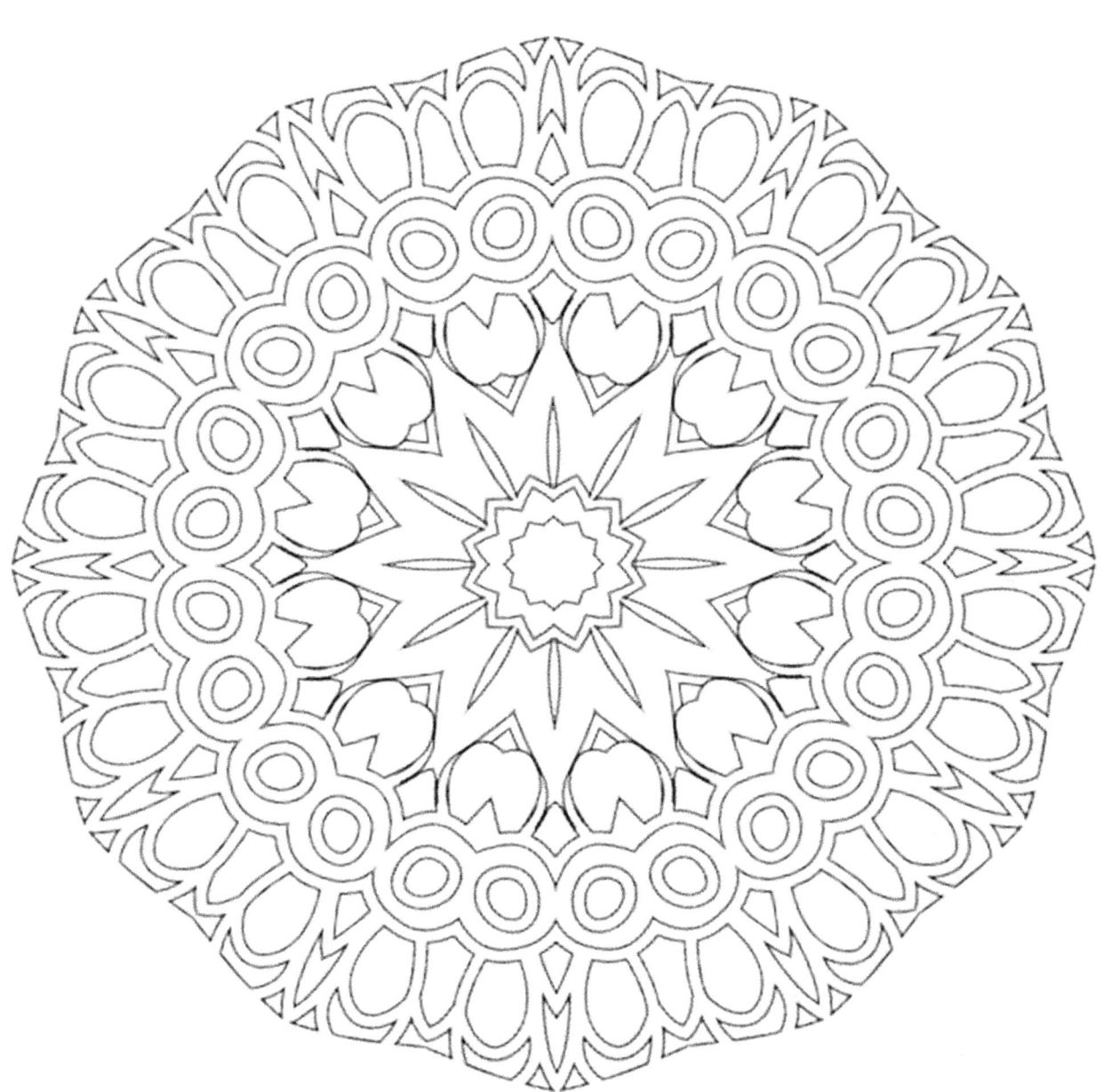

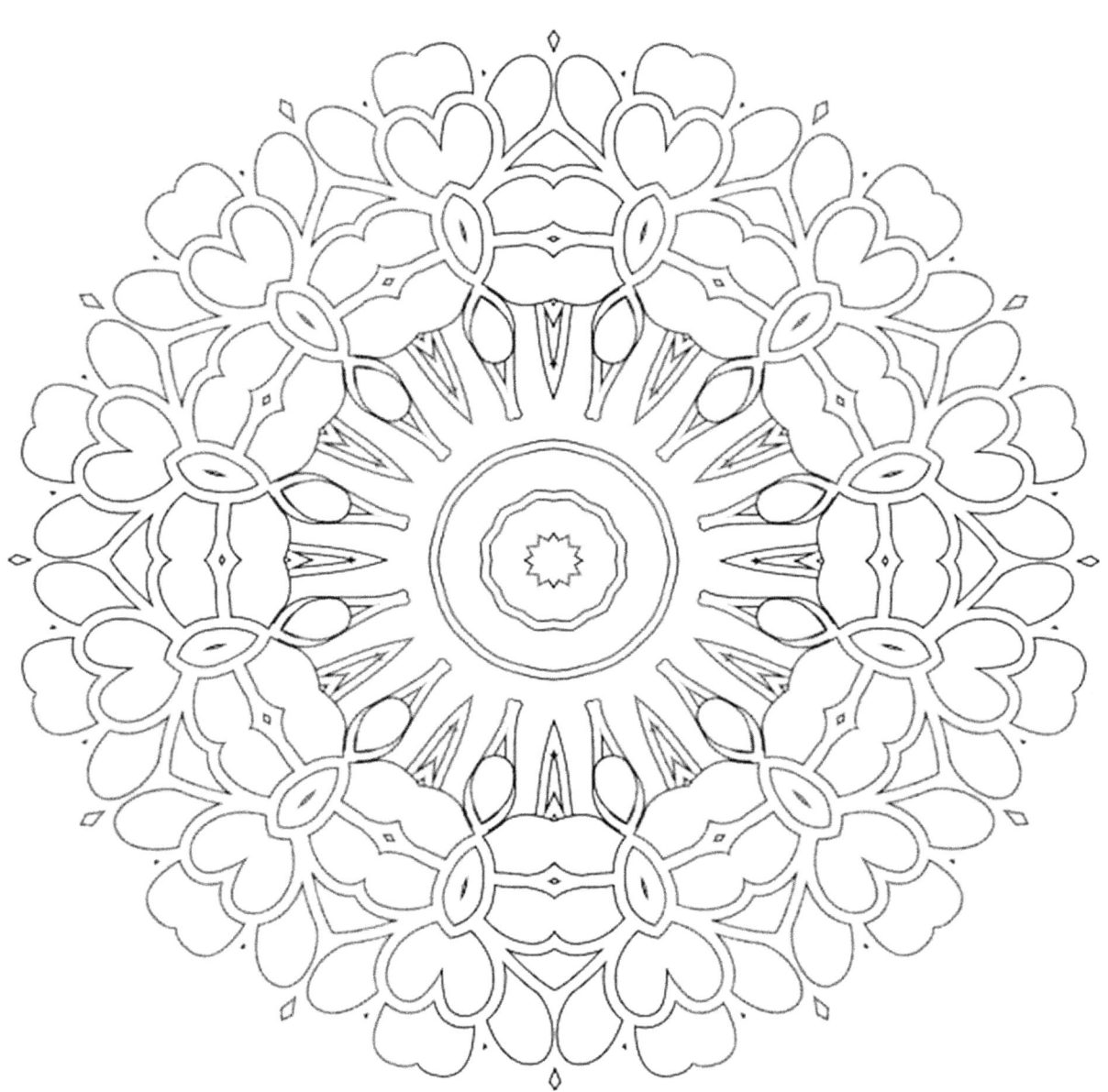

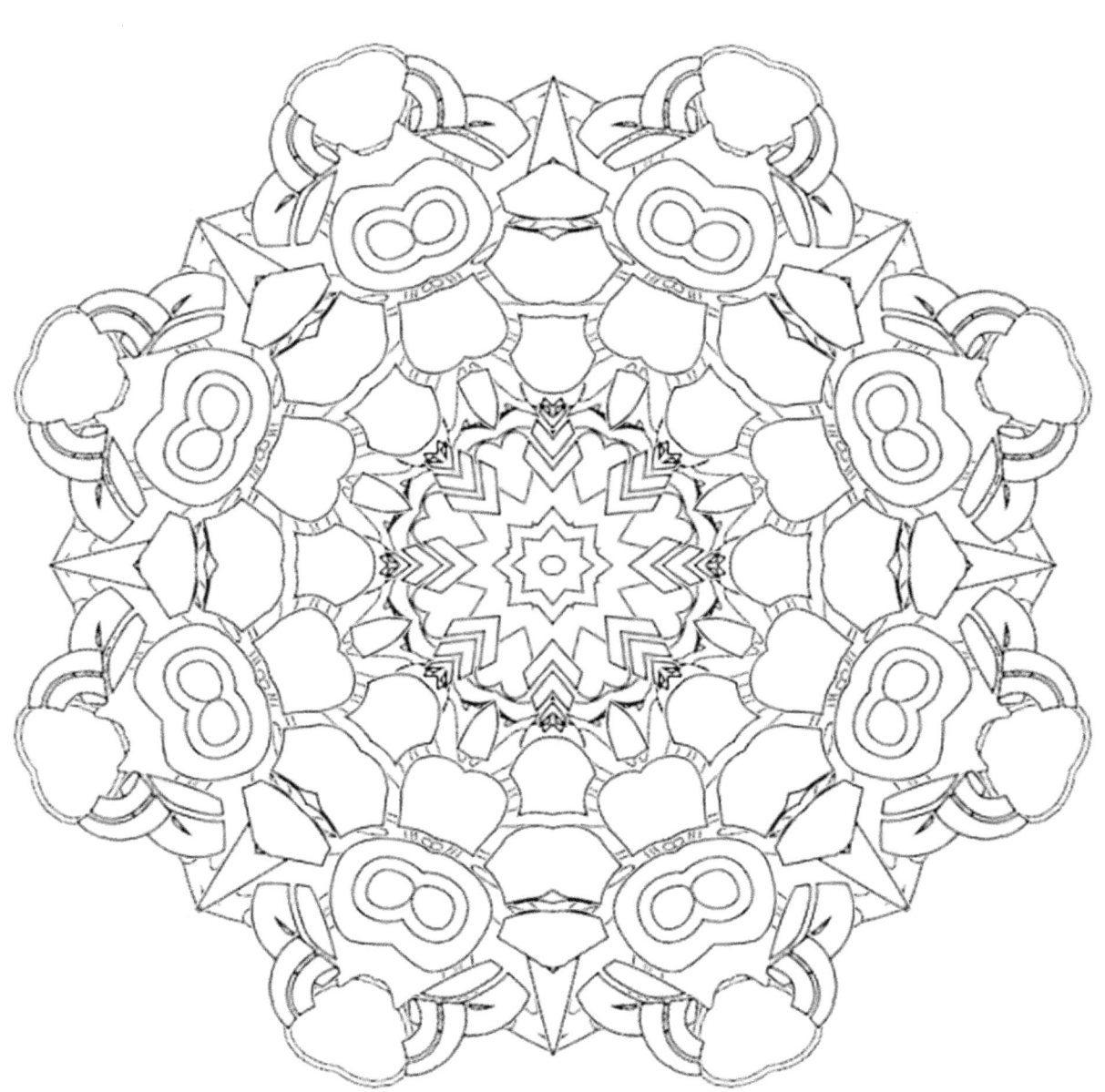

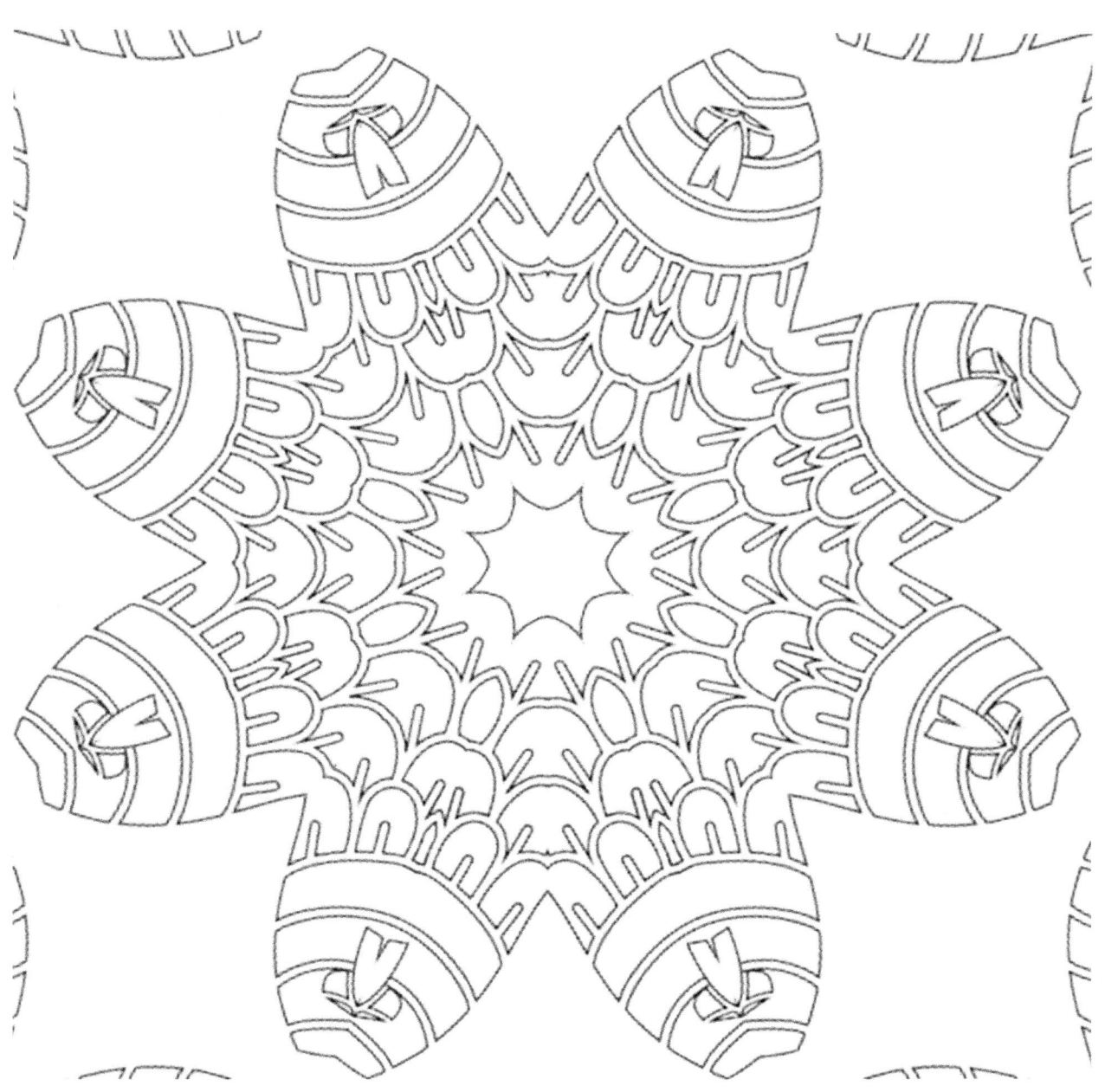

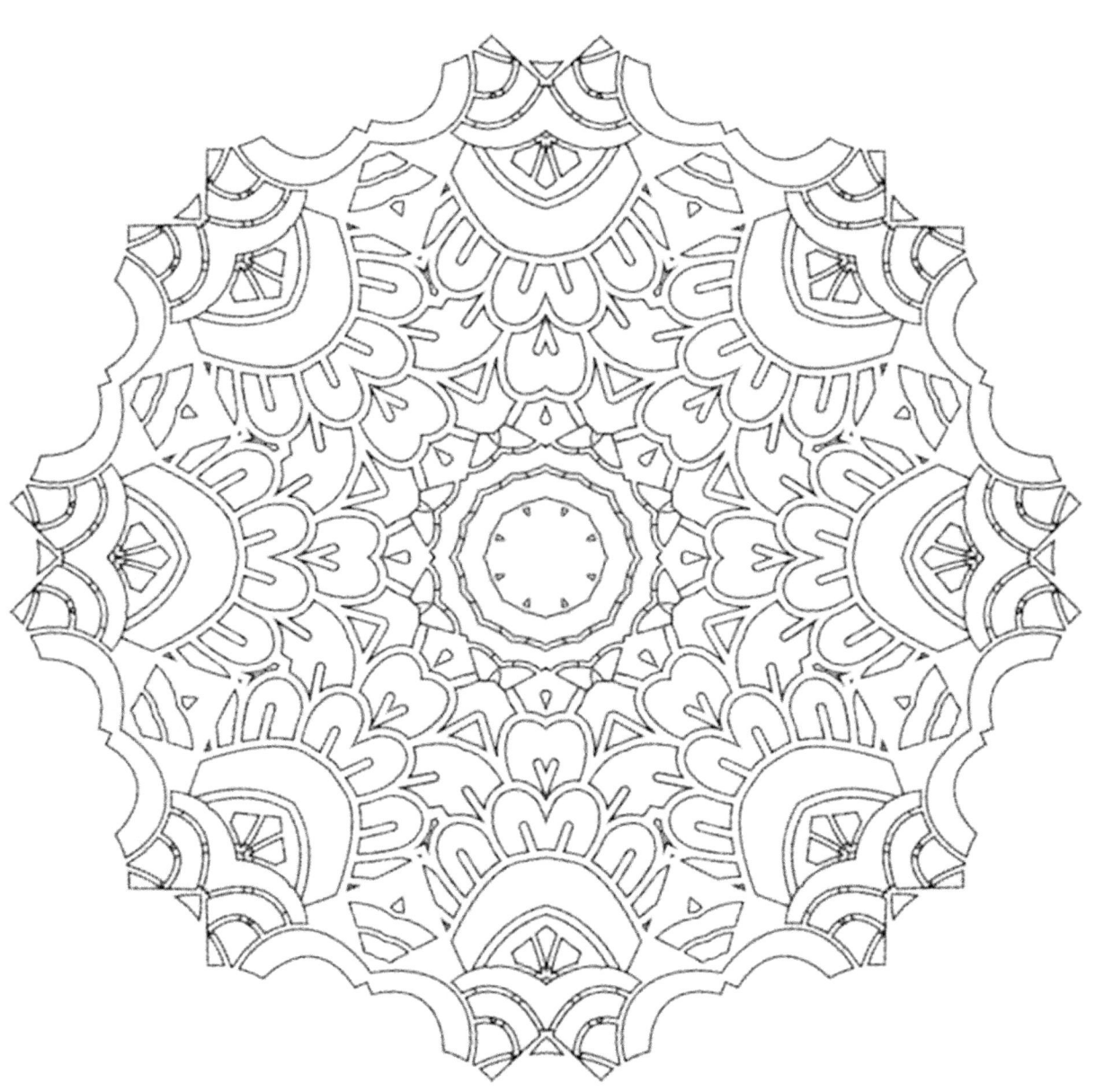

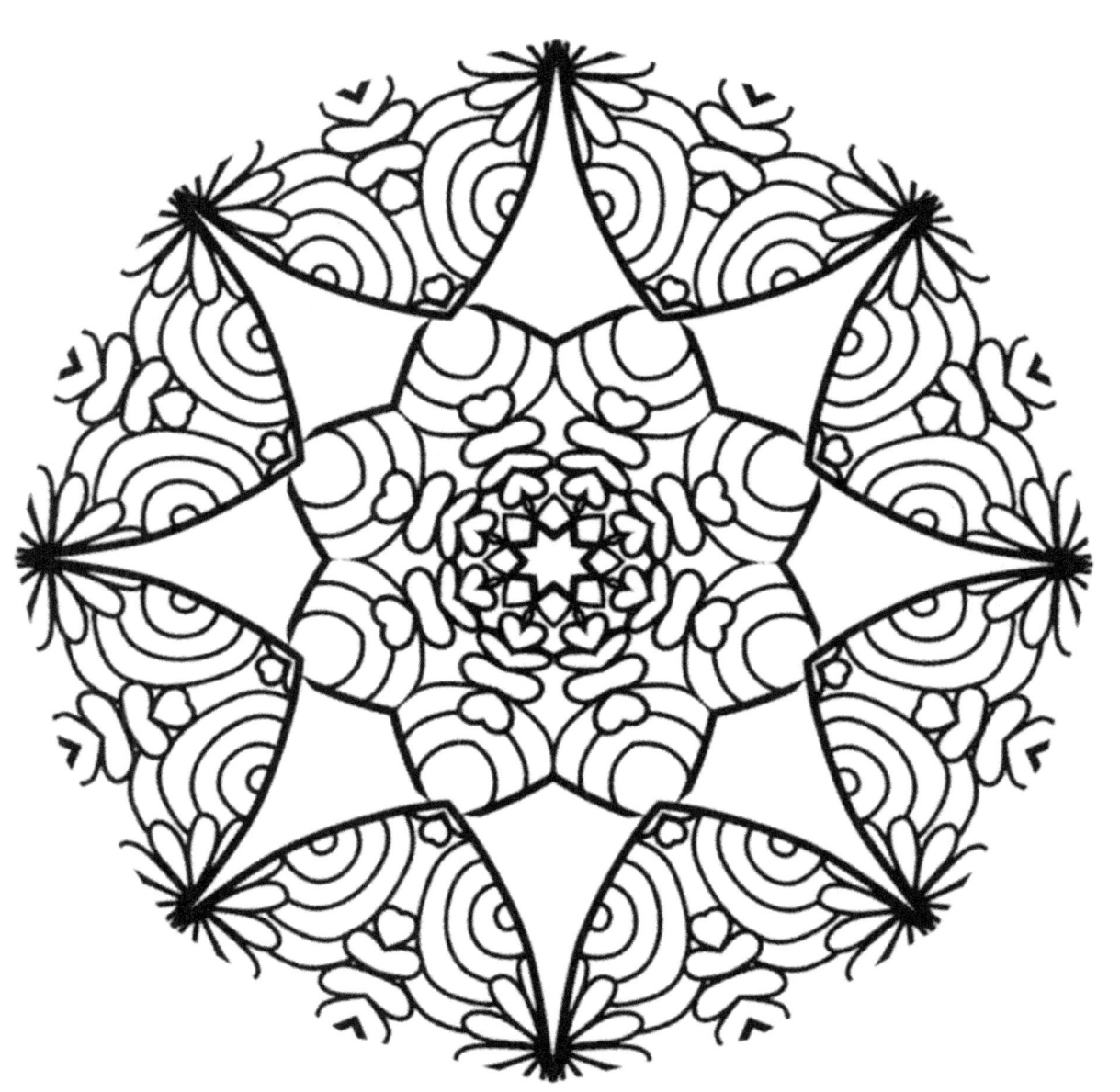

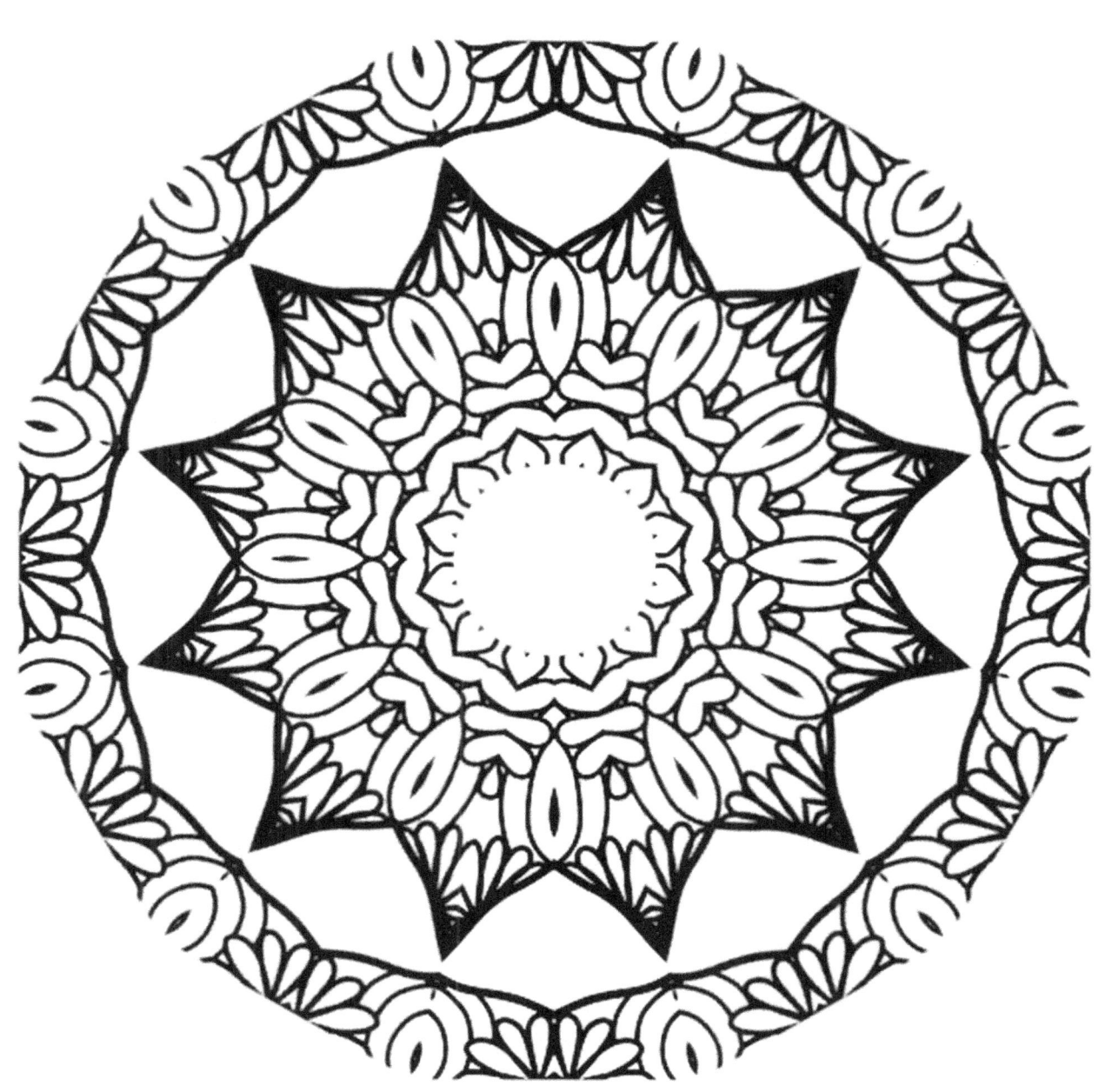

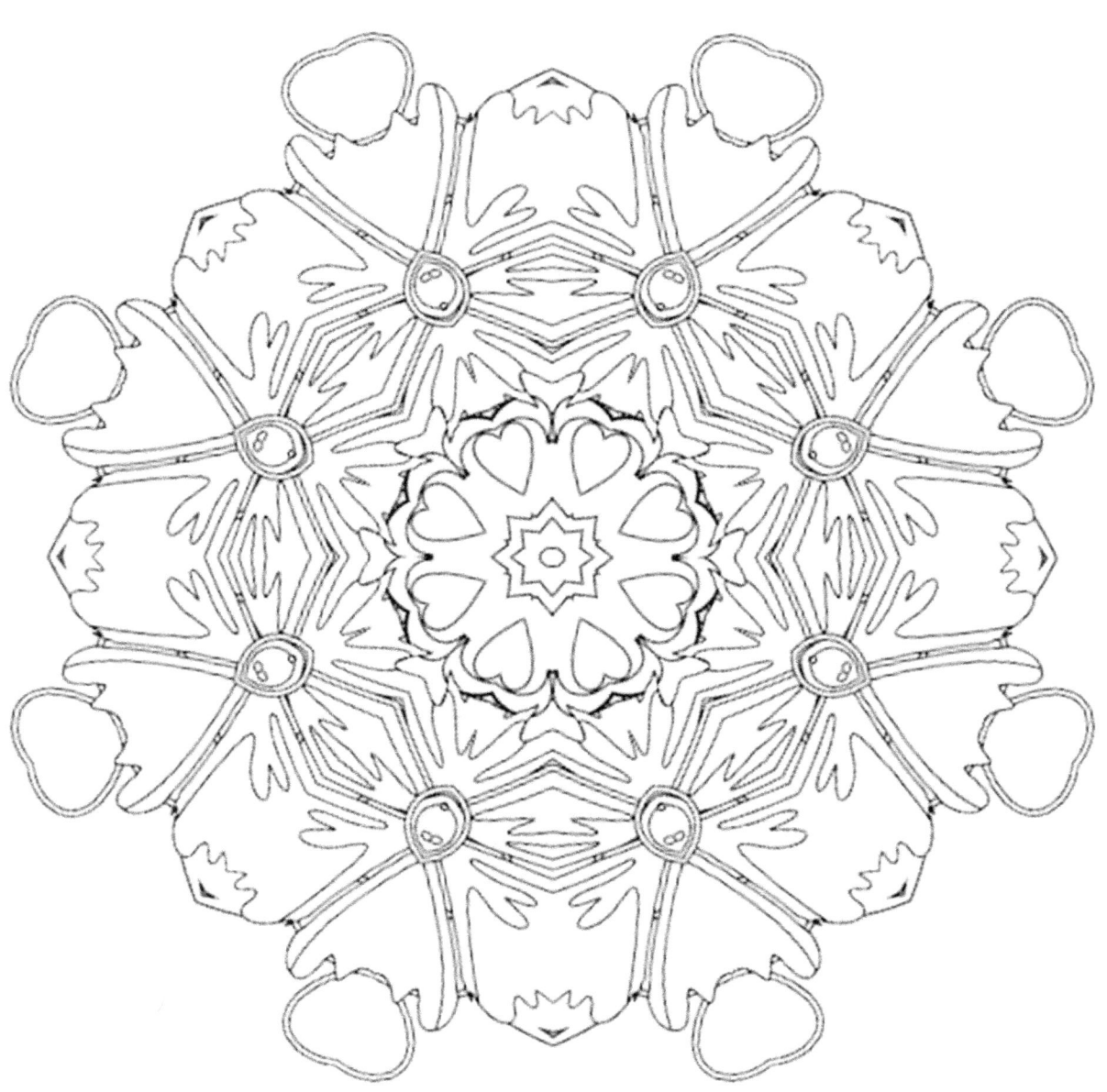

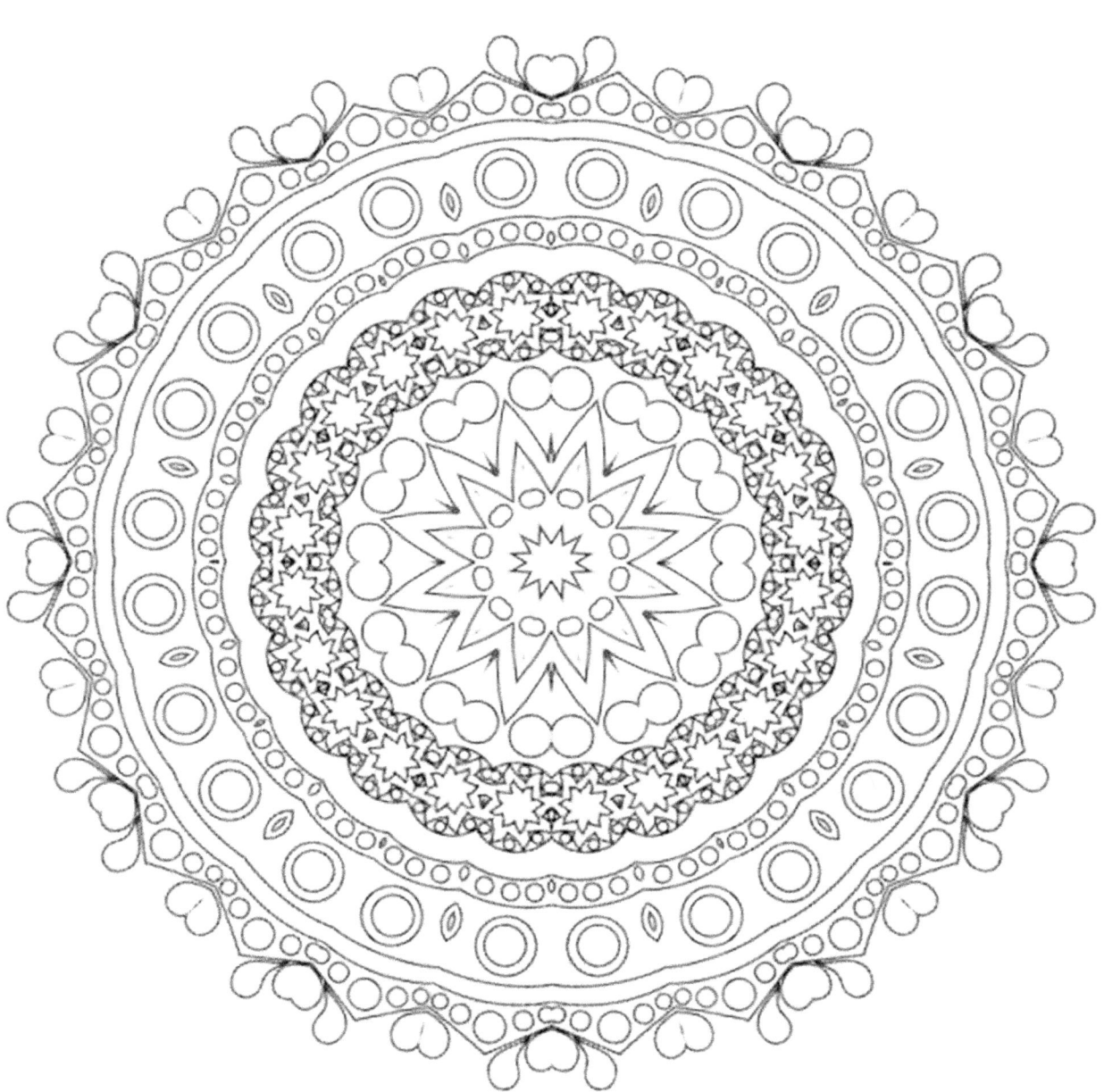

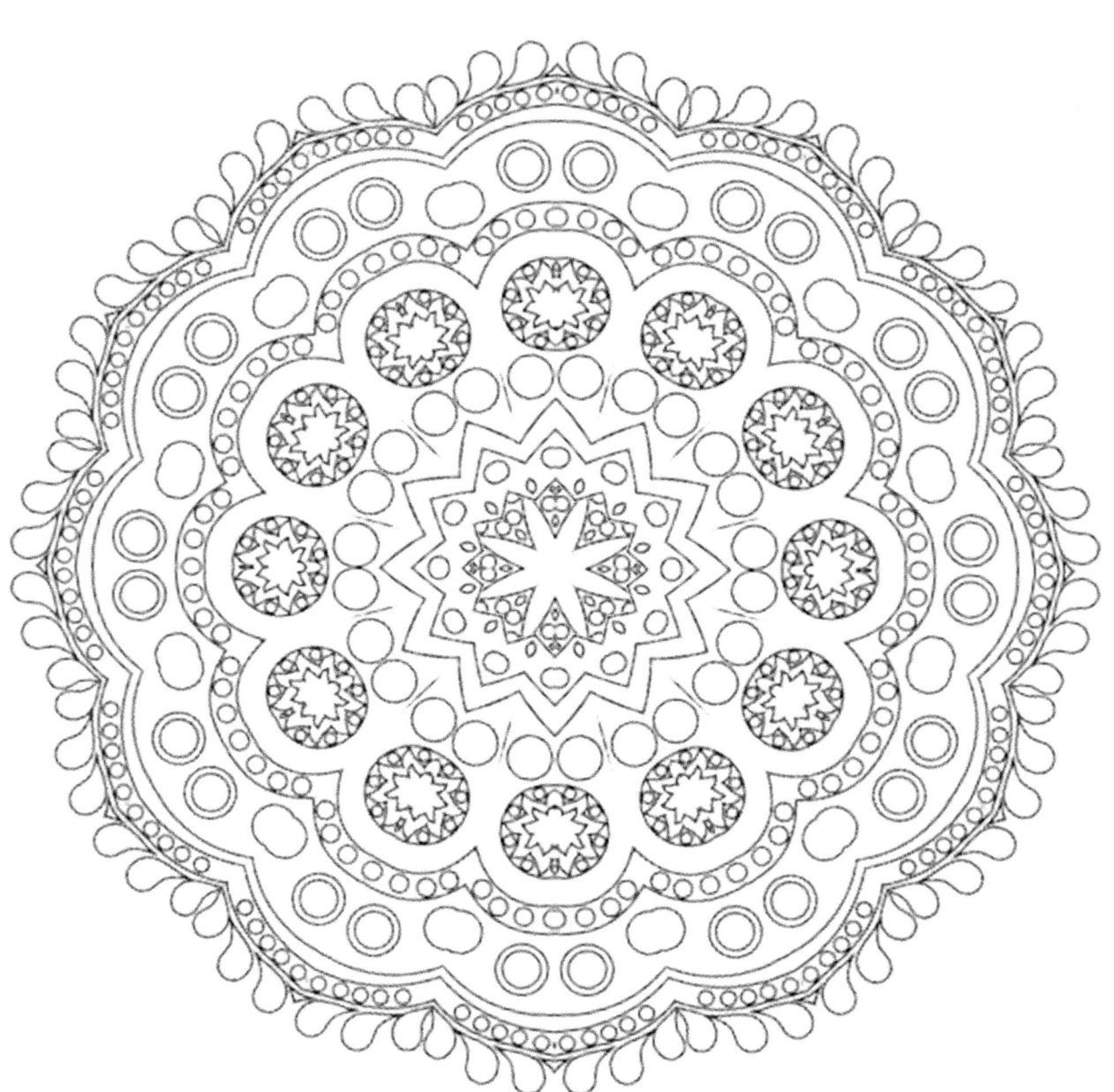

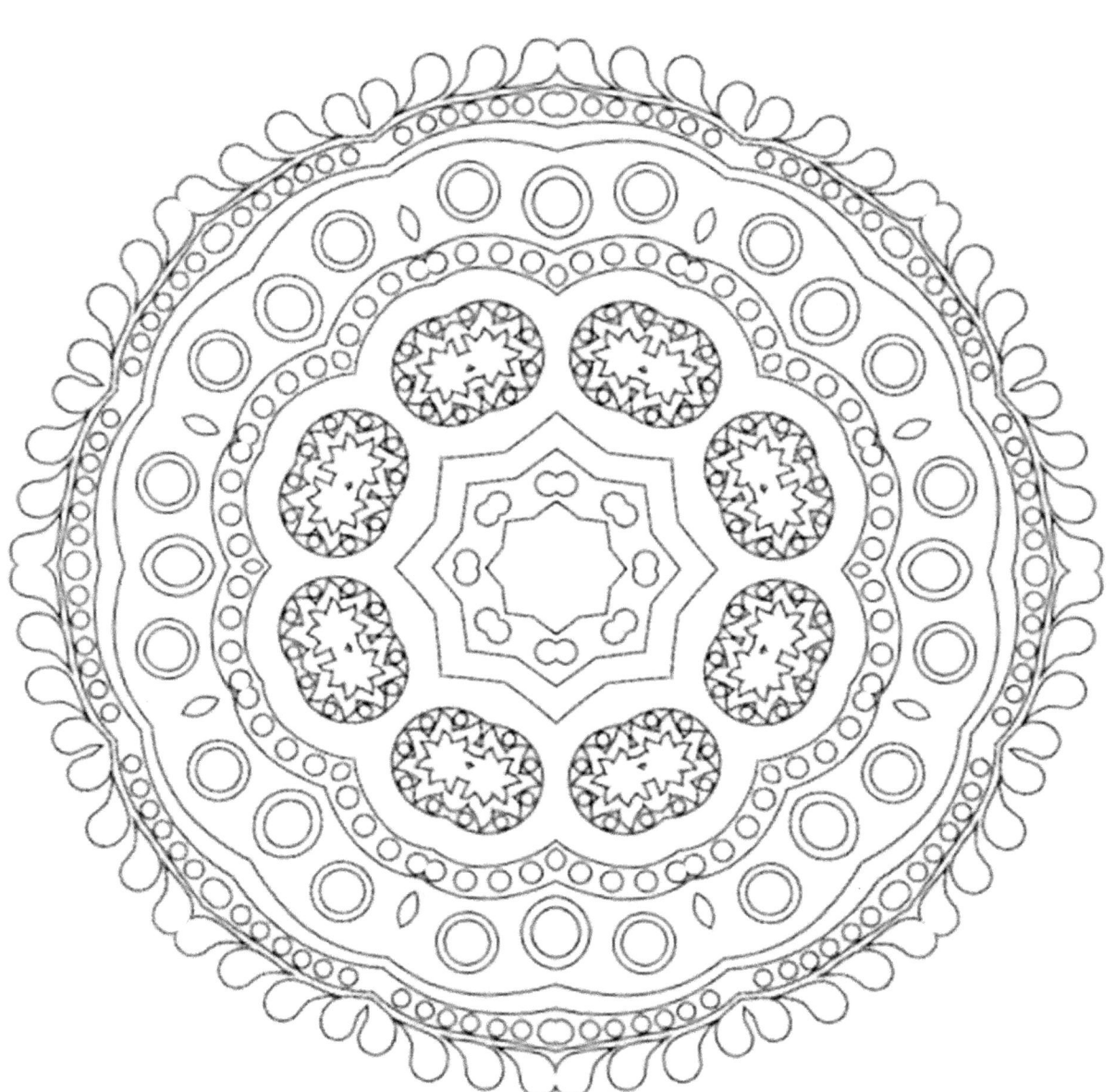

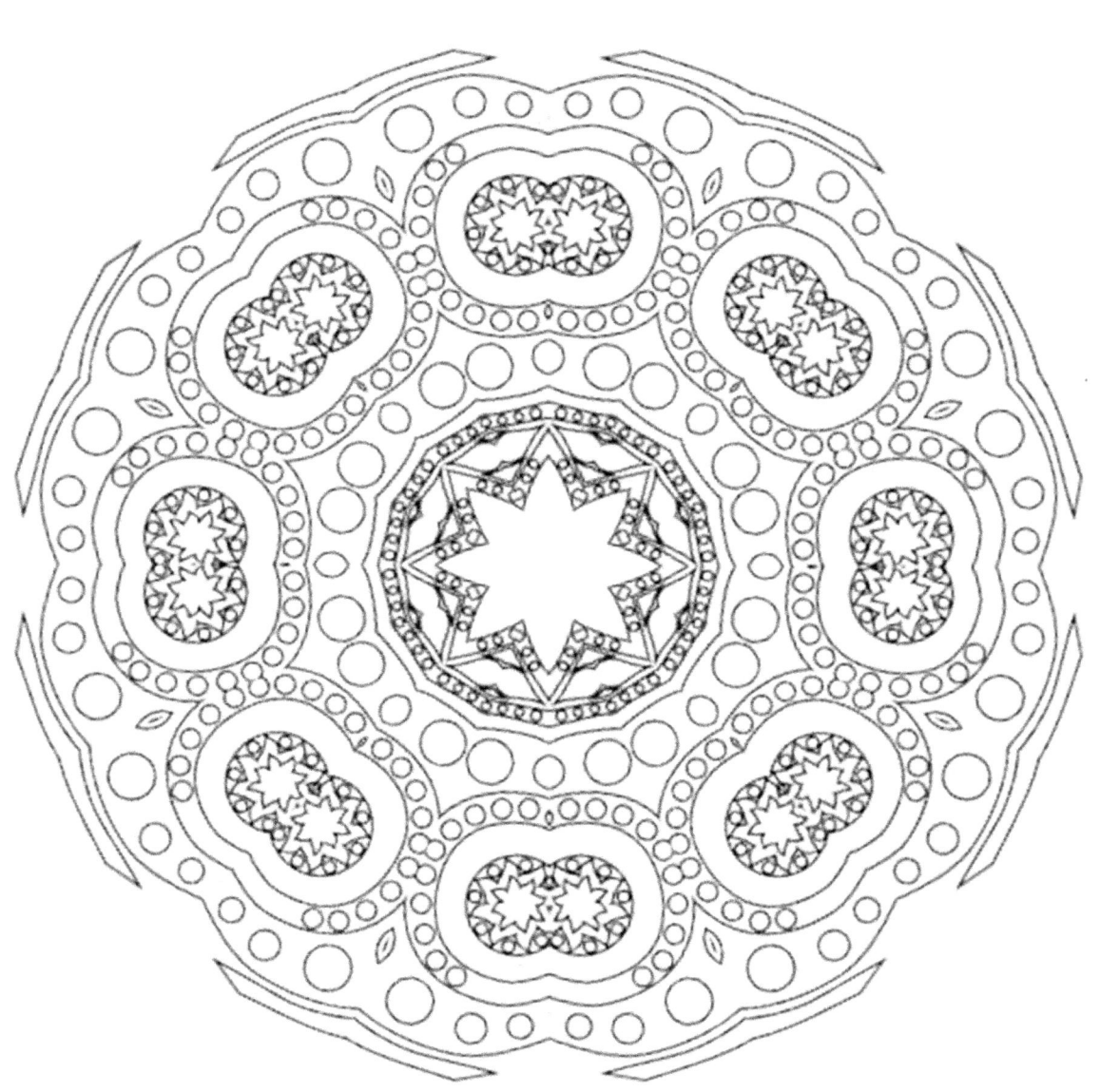

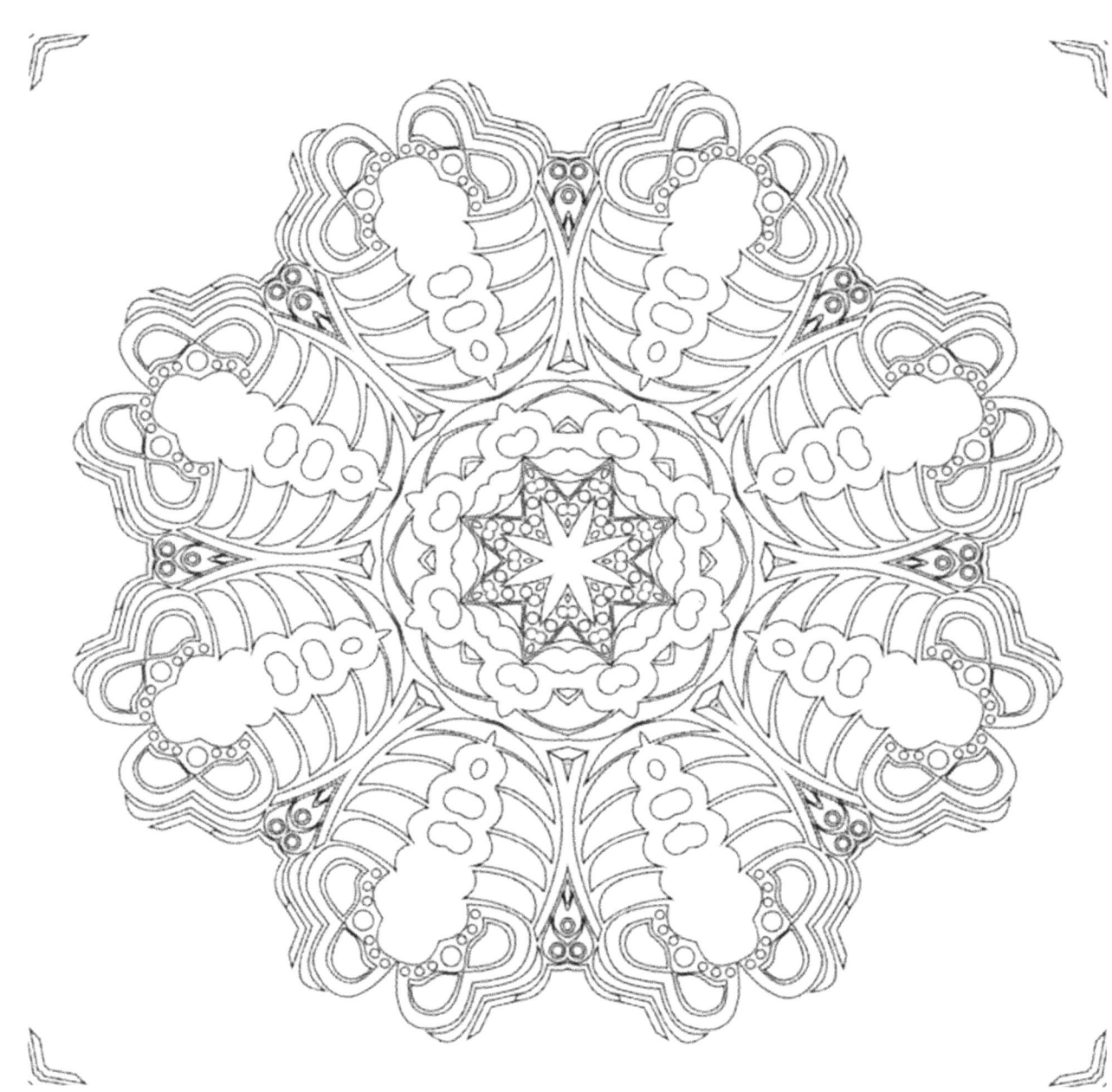

www.ingramcontent.com/pod-product-compliance
Lightning Source LLC
Chambersburg PA
CBHW081751280526
45789CB00008B/2817